CELEBRATIONS

OUR
JEWISH
HOLIDAYS

CELEBRATIONS

OUR
JEWISH
HOLIDAYS

written and illustrated by
MELANIE HOPE GREENBERG

The Jewish Publication Society
Philadelphia - New York
5752 - 1991

Library of Congress Cataloging-in-Publication Data
Greenberg, Melanie Hope.
        Celebrations : Our Jewish holidays / written and illustrated by
    Melanie Hope Greenberg.
            p. cm.
        Summary: Provides brief descriptions of thirteen major Jewish
    holidays.
        ISBN 0-8276-0396-7
        1. Fasts and Feasts—Judaism—Juvenile literature. [1. Fasts and
    Feasts—Judaism.]   I. Title.
    BM690.G69   1991
    296.4'3—dc20   91-12744
                                                              CIP
                                                               AC

10 9 8 7 6 5 4 3 2 1

To all people and their traditions

SHABBAT

God made day and night,

the sky and the sea,

the trees, the animals,

and us.

God rested after six days of creation,

and so do we.

Shabbat is my favorite holiday

because it comes every week.

ROSH HASHANA

Ta-ki-ya-u, Ta-ki-ru-ah
blows the shofar.
We all pray
for a happy new year.

YOM KIPPUR

Mommy and Daddy
pray and fast all day.
I pray too.
God bless Mommy and Daddy,
my aunts and uncles,
my cousins and friends,
and me.
At sundown we have
breakfast for dinner.

SUKKOT

Daddy picks me up
so I can tie big, shiny apples
to the roof of the sukkah.
I helped build ours.
I look up at the stars
and remember the Jews who
traveled through the desert
after they left slavery
in Egypt.

SIMCHAT TORAH

Hooray for the Torah!

We clap and sing and dance.

I wave my flag.

Someday I will read the Torah!

CHANUKAH

For eight nights we light
candles in the menorah and
remember how hard the Jews
fought for the freedom
to live and pray as Jews.
I love to watch the lights
dance in the window.

TU BISHVAT

Happy New Year to the trees!

I planted a seed.

Mommy said, "Wait and see."

I hope the seed will

grow as big as the tree outside my window.

PURIM

We listen to the Megillah.
We boo and stamp our feet
and make noise
every time we hear wicked
Haman's name.
Hooray for Queen Esther and Mordecai,
who saved the Jews from Haman.

PESACH

Why is this night different
from all other nights?
The Jews were slaves in Egypt.
Tonight we drink wine and
eat matzah
and remember that God helped us to
become free.

YOM HASHOAH

Sometimes bad things
happen in the world.
Daddy says the Holocaust
was the worst bad thing.
So many people were killed just
because they were Jews.

YOM HA'ATZMA'UT

After two thousand years,
the Jews have their own country again.
Happy Birthday to Israel,
the land of the Jewish people!

SHAVUOT

I helped Mommy pick flowers.
This one is for you, Mommy,
and this one is for God.
Thank you, God, for giving us the
Ten Commandments and
the holy Torah.

TISHAH BE'AV

We sit around the campfire
and hear the sad story
of the destruction of the
Temple in Jerusalem.
We all hope and pray
for a better future.